DIVORCE COLORING BOOK

CRYSTAL
COLORING BOOKS

Copyright © 2018 Crystal Coloring Books
All rights reserved.
ISBN-10: 1986171469

ISBN-13: 978-1986619615
ISBN-10: 1986619613

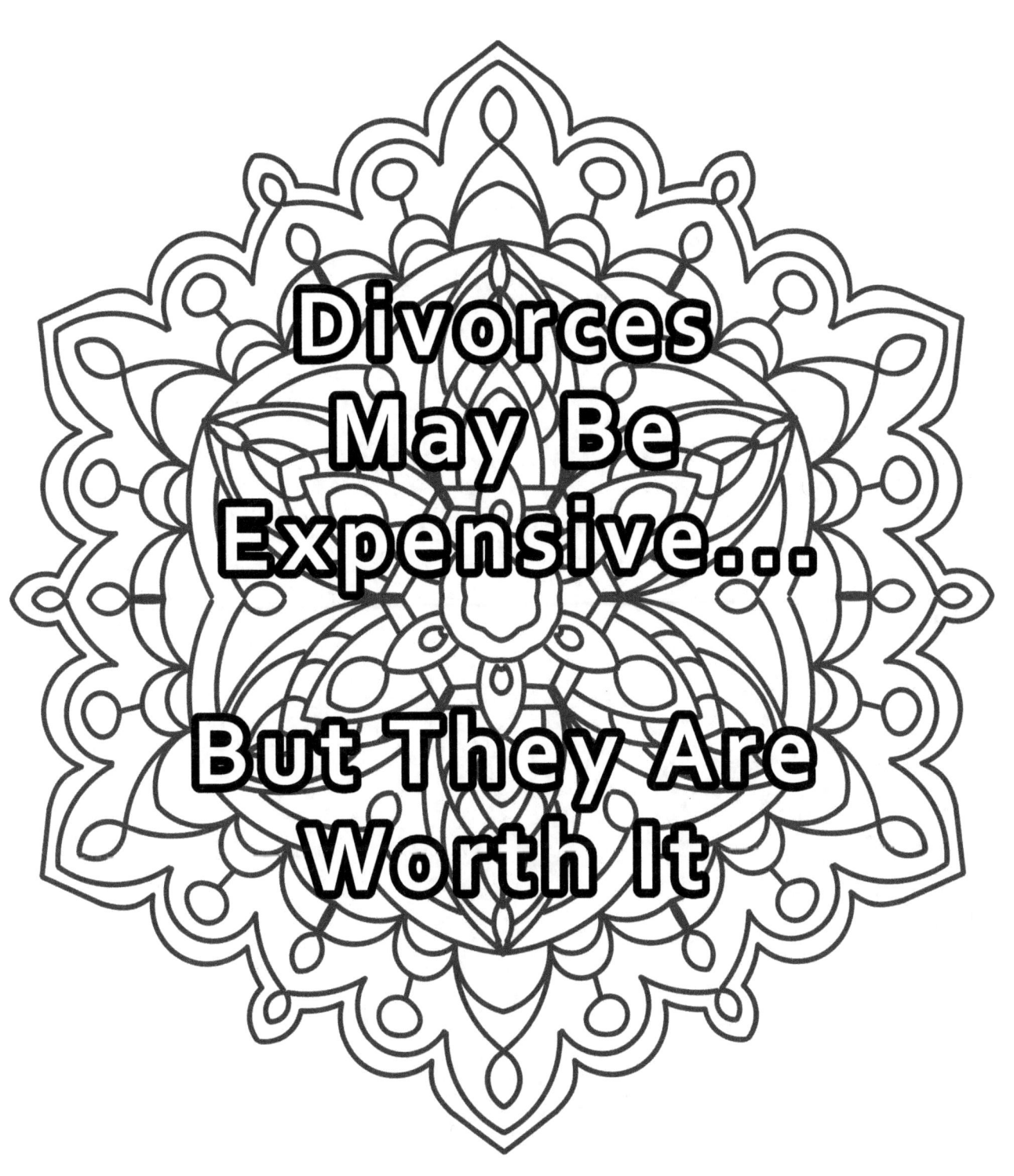

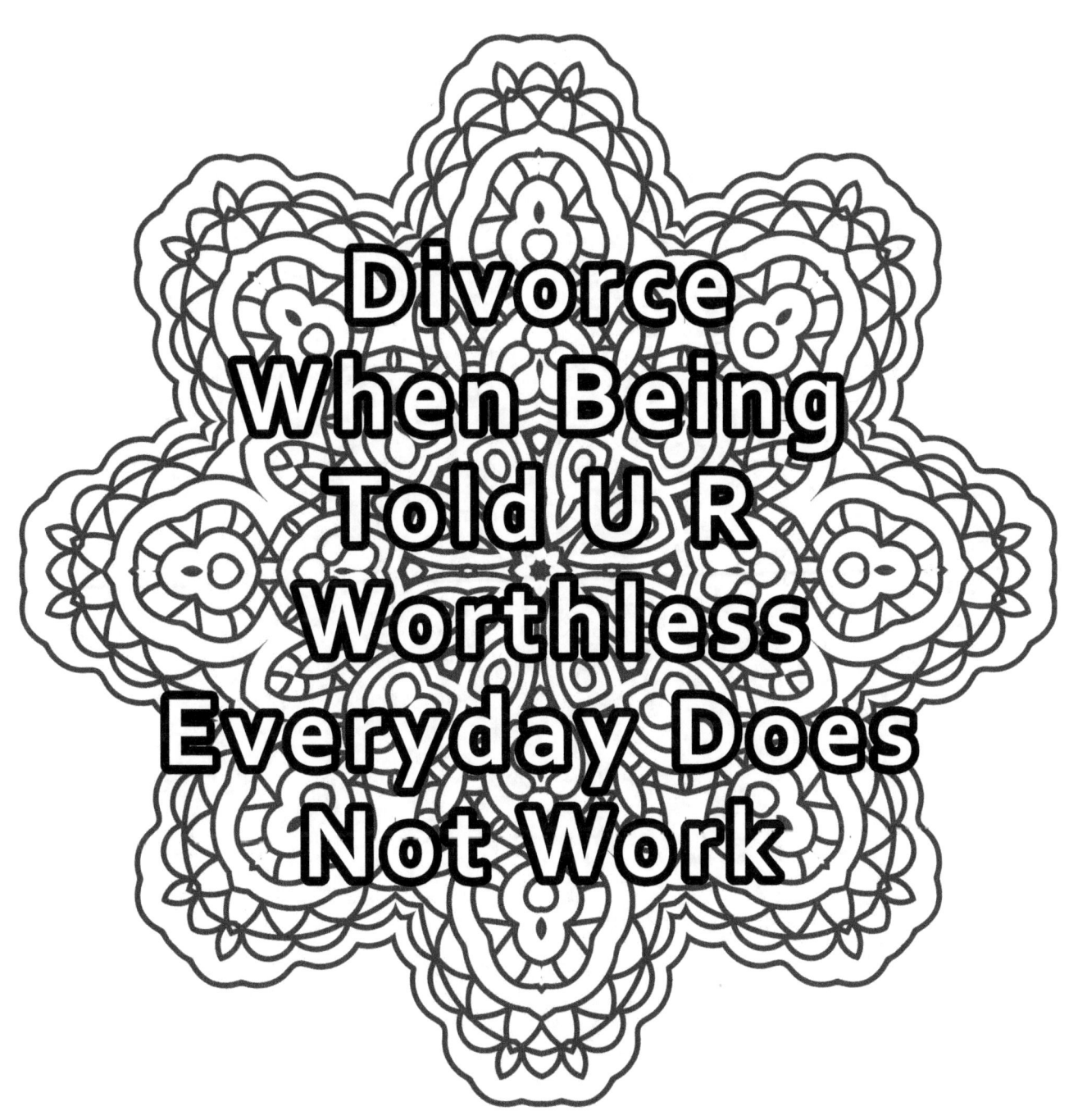

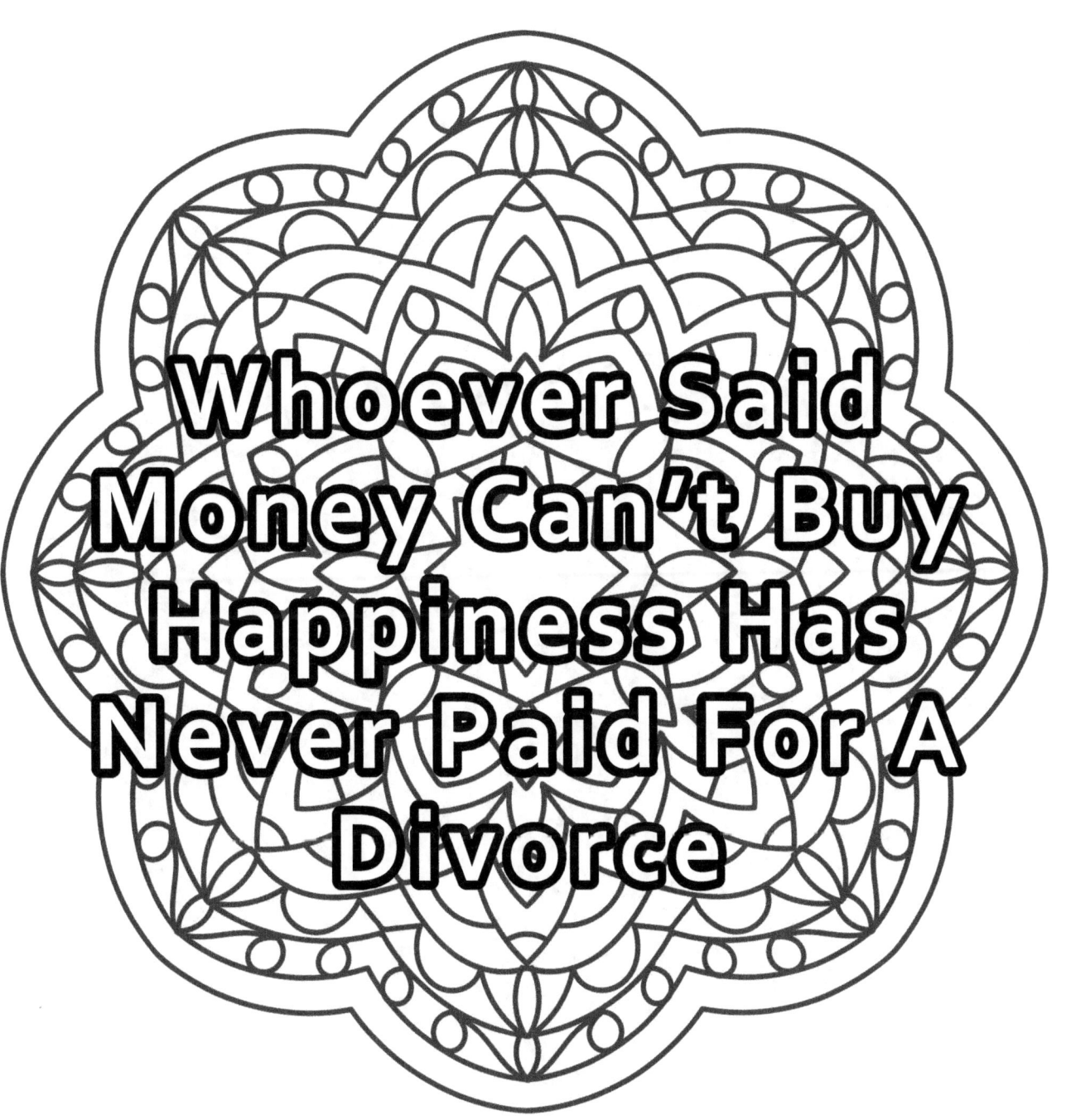

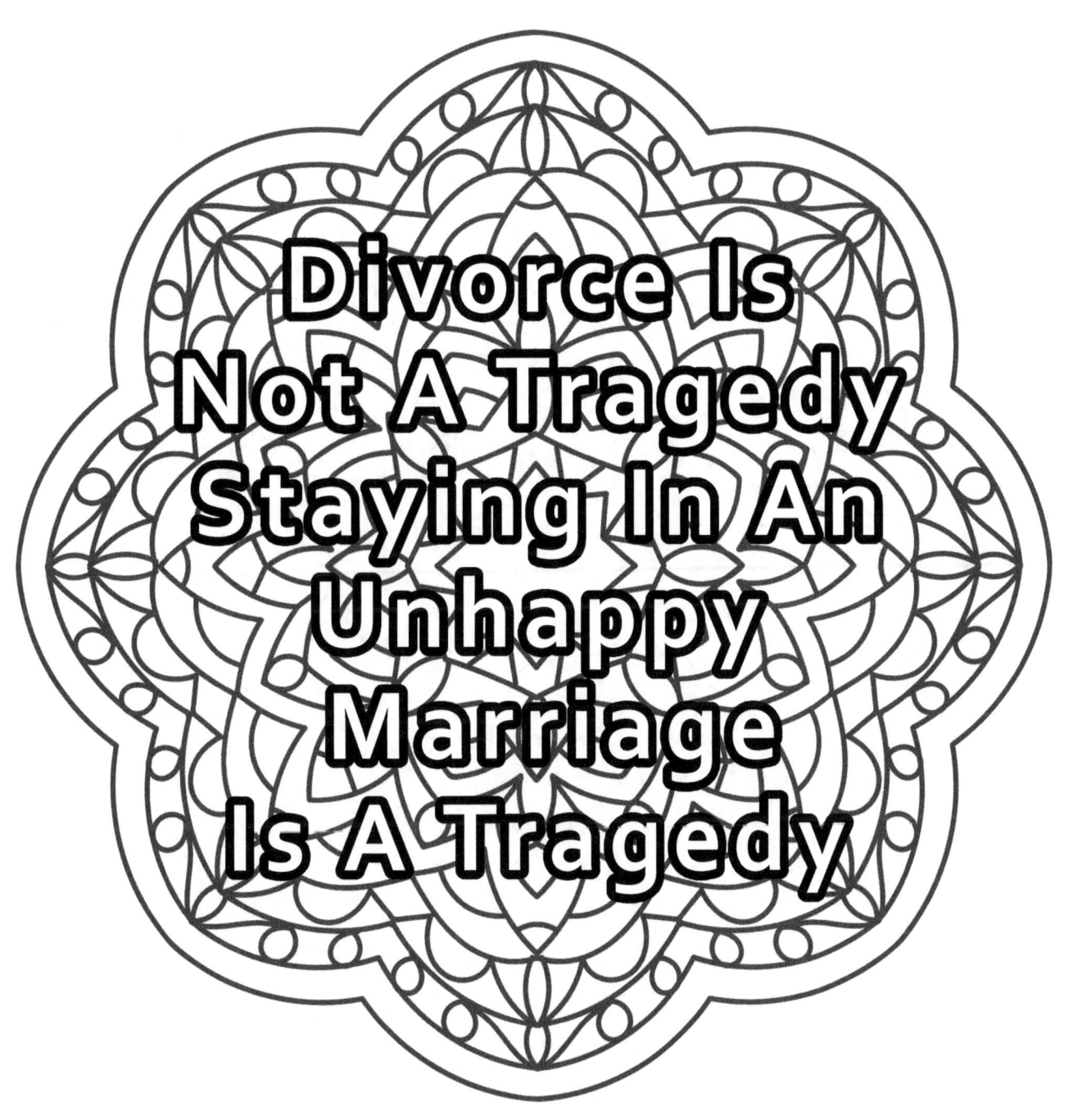

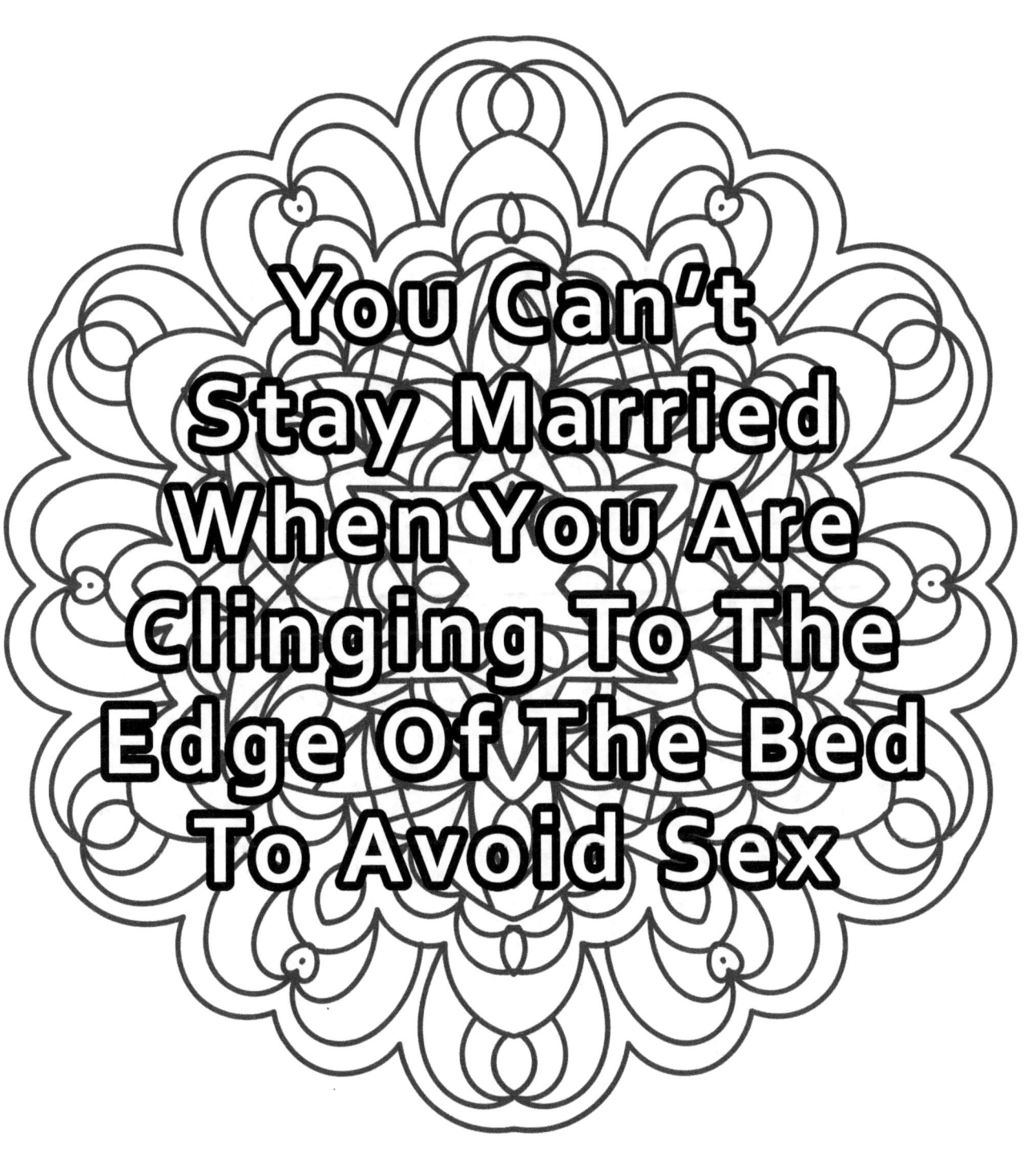

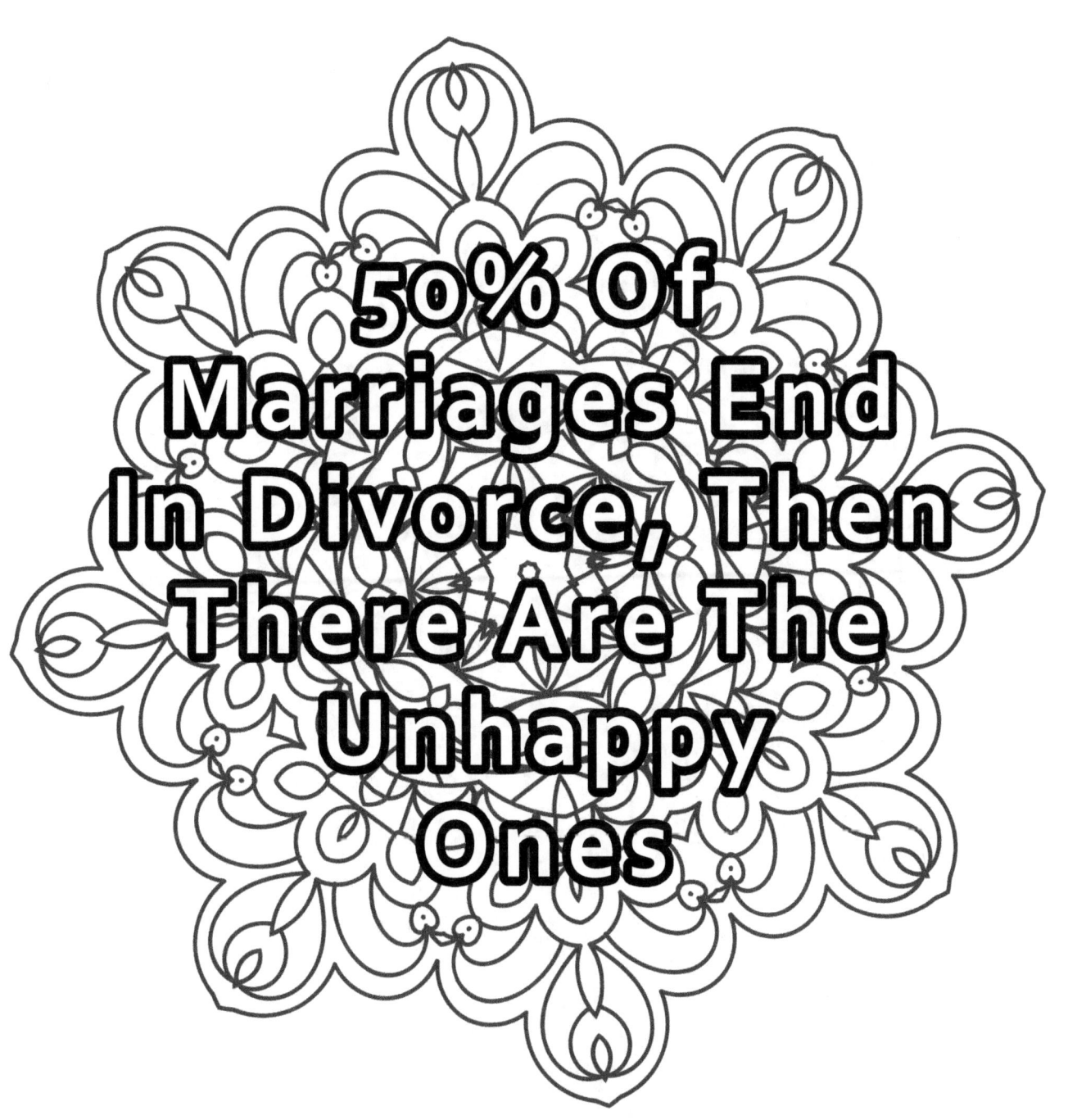

A Friend Divorced His Wife. He Said He Was Looking For A 'Some Sex Marriage'

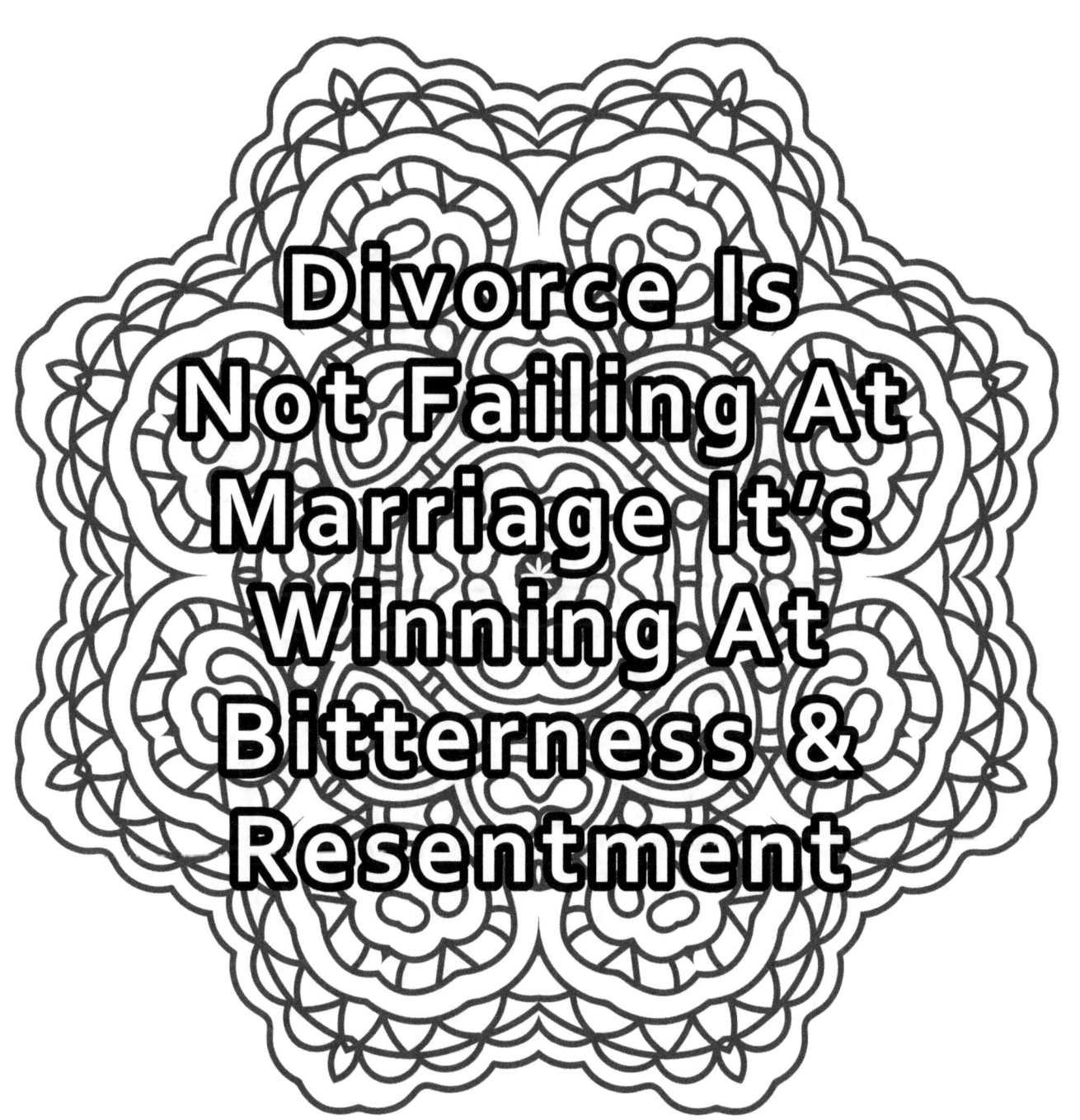

COLOR TEST PAGE

www.ingramcontent.com/pod-product-compliance
Lightning Source LLC
Chambersburg PA
CBHW062126220526
45471CB00010B/3906